Page Turners

The Choice

Sue Leather

Series Editors:
Rob Waring and Sue Leather
Series Story Consultant: Julian Thomlinson
Story Editor: Julian Thomlinson

NATIONAL GEOGRAPHIC LEARNING | CENGAGE Learning

Australia • Brazil • Japan • Korea • Mexico • Singapore • Spain • United Kingdom • United States

NATIONAL GEOGRAPHIC LEARNING | CENGAGE Learning

Page Turners Reading Library

The Choice

Sue Leather

Publisher: Andrew Robinson

Executive Editor: Sean Bermingham

Editorial Assistant: Dylan Mitchell

Director of Global Marketing: Ian Martin

Senior Content Project Manager: Tan Jin Hock

Manufacturing Planner: Mary Beth Hennebury

Contributors: Vessela Gasper, Jessie Chew

Layout Design and Illustrations: Redbean Design Pte Ltd

Cover Illustration: Eric Foenander

ISBN-13: 978-1-4240-4655-3

ISBN-10: 1-4240-4655-6

National Geographic Learning
20 Channel Center Street
Boston, Massachusetts 02210
USA

Cengage Learning is a leading provider of customized learning solutions with office locations around the globe, including Singapore, the United Kingdom, Australia, Mexico, Brazil, and Japan.

Cengage Learning products are represented in Canada by Nelson Education, Ltd.

Visit National Geographic Learning online at **NGL.Cengage.com**

Visit our corporate website at **www.cengage.com**

Printed in the United States of America
2 3 4 5 6 7 8 24 23 22 21 20

Contents

People in the story

Anna Mason
a 29-year-old computer science student, just graduating from Cambridge University

Joe Mason
Anna's husband, who works in an electrical appliances store

Lisa Bridges
a 21-year-old computer science student and a friend of Anna

The story is set in Cambridge, England.

Chapter 1

A visit

"Wow, he's absolutely beautiful!" Anna looked at her nephew Billy, lying in his little bed. His little face was red. *It's funny how babies can be kind of ugly and beautiful all at the same time,* she thought.

Anna's husband, Joe, agreed. "He *is* lovely," he said.

Anna and Joe were at Joe's brother's house to see their new baby.

"Well done, you two!" Joe congratulated his brother, Chris, and his wife, Lyn.

Chris and Lyn smiled. "Thanks!" said Chris. "Two girls and a boy now. That's it, isn't it, love?"

"Yes! Absolutely!" Lyn laughed. "More than enough."

Their two little girls, Clara and Lizzie, were four and five years old. At the moment, they were running around the bedroom. They laughed and shouted as they ran. Joe was playing with them.

"Shh . . . , be quiet you two. Mommy's tired, and little Billy's asleep!" Chris said. "In fact, it's your bedtime, too!"

"Awww!!" The two little girls were not happy.

"Here," said Joe. "I'll put them to bed, Chris. Come on, you two."

Clara and Lizzie each took hold of one of Joe's hands and screamed, "Uncle Joe! Uncle Joe!"

"Thanks, Joe," said Chris.

Joe took the two little girls to their room to put them to bed. When he came out, the four adults went downstairs.

"I just wish Mom and Dad were here to see him. Well, all of the kids," Chris said, as they sat down to dinner.

"Yeah," Joe smiled sadly. Their parents had had Joe and Chris when they were older, and they'd died before Chris's children were born. "They would love having grandchildren," he added.

There was silence for a moment or two.

"Anyway," Anna said, finally. "Here's to little Billy!" She lifted her glass, and the other three followed her. "To Billy!" they all said.

At around 10 o'clock, Anna and Joe left to go home. Joe had work in the morning, and Anna had to go to the university. As they drove, Anna talked about baby Billy and how happy Chris and Lyn seemed. "Those are three lovely kids," she said. "Billy's gorgeous, isn't he?"

Joe didn't answer. She looked across at him. He was watching the road carefully as he drove across the city, but she saw that he didn't look happy.

"What's the matter?" she asked. "You look miserable. Didn't you enjoy yourself at Chris's?"

"Oh it's not that . . ." said Joe.

"Well, what is it?"

"I . . . oh, nothing, I guess . . ."

"Well, it must be something, Joe," Anna said. "Come on." But Joe didn't say anything all the way home.

◇◇◇

The next day at the university, Anna tried to just think about her work. She was almost at the end of her three years at Cambridge University now, and soon she would graduate. Cambridge! Sometimes she still couldn't believe she was studying here. But she was, and her computer science course was everything she wanted. The other students in the course were great, too. At twenty-nine, Anna was older than all of them, but she'd made some really good friends. It didn't seem to make any difference to them that she was older, and married.

"Hey, come and have a look at this before you go," said her friend Lisa. Anna went over to look at Lisa's computer. Lisa and Anna were working with another student, Ella, on a special software project to help doctors. The three of them wanted to develop the idea more when they graduated. Anna wanted to work on computers more than anything.

"I really think this is interesting, Anna," said Lisa. "And I was talking to Professor Jensen. She thinks we can get some money from the university and maybe some from a company. We can develop it to sell! It means we're going to be really busy for at least three years after we graduate."

"Three years! That's great!" said Anna, smiling at her friend. "Let's talk to Ella about it tomorrow."

"OK," said Lisa. "Have a great evening, Anna, and give my love to Joe."

Anna walked away from the computer laboratory, toward the bus stop.

She waited for the number 36 bus. It was nearly the end of April, but a cold wind still blew off the fens, the flat land that lay all around the city of Cambridge. Anna was happy when the blue and white bus came along. She sat down and looked out the window. She thought about the project. The idea of working on it after graduating was really exciting! *What will Joe think about it?,* she wondered.

Chapter 2

A discussion

Joe greeted his wife as she came into the living room of their small, comfortable home. "Hi, love! You're a bit late. How was it?"

"Good," she said. "Great, in fact. How was work?" She kissed him.

Joe worked at an electrical appliances store in the city. He'd worked there since he left school at sixteen. A year older than his wife, he was tall and athletic. He was a friendly kind of guy who had lots of friends. People liked him.

"Oh, you know, same as ever." Joe smiled. "The usual crazy customers. There was this one guy who came in to return a TV he'd bought. He was really angry, shouting and everything. But it turned out he'd bought it at a different store!"

Anna laughed as she sat down on the sofa next to Joe. "Really?"

"Yeah, really," Joe said.

She looked at him closely. "I'm sure some of your stories aren't true," Anna said. She and Joe first met when Anna was sixteen and Joe was seventeen. They knew each other really well.

"No, really. It's true," Joe said. "You should have seen the guy's face when we told him!" They both laughed.

"So, what about you?" asked Joe. "What did you do today?"

"Well, we were working on our project, you know, me, Lisa, and Ella—Lisa says hi, by the way—and it's going pretty well. In fact, Professor Jensen thinks it may be good enough to develop and sell." Anna's face was happy. "It looks like I'll have a lot of work with our project . . ."

"Oh?"

"Yes," said Anna. "About three years' work, in fact, with money to develop it."

Joe stopped smiling.

"What's wrong?"

"Oh . . . nothing," said Joe, "but three years!"

"Well, yes . . ." Anna said. She looked at her husband. "But it's OK, isn't it?" she asked.

"Sure," said Joe. He kissed his wife on the head. "My clever Anna," he added. Then he got up and went to the kitchen to make tea.

When he came back with the tea, Joe wasn't smiling.

"It isn't OK, is it?" Anna asked.

"I . . ."

"Joe?"

Joe didn't speak.

"Come on," said Anna. "I could see you weren't happy last night. What's wrong?"

Joe put the teacups on the little table and sat down.

"Well," he said, finally, "I've been thinking about it for a while, Anna. And seeing the kids yesterday . . . well, it made me think, you know." He didn't look at Anna, but stared at the wall.

"What?"

"Well, you know, Mom and Dad had me and Chris quite late."

"I know . . ."

"And then," Joe went on, "they . . . well, they never saw us as adults." He turned to look at her. "I . . . I don't want that to happen to us, Anna."

"So that's it," Anna said as she sat down. "That's what you're thinking about."

Joe and Anna both knew they wanted children. But they decided that they would have them later. Anna wanted to go to university and then start a "real" career before having a baby. Joe had agreed that it was the best idea.

"But we discussed all this a long time ago, darling," Anna said.

"I know we did, Anna," said Joe, sitting down next to his wife. "But, I don't know . . . seeing Chris and Lyn . . . I just feel like it's best for us to have our kids when we're young. I mean, I want to see them become grown-ups, have their own kids . . ."

"And now," he went on, "you're leaving university, but you're going to go on with this project, and it's going to be at least three years before you can have children. You're twenty-nine now; that means you'll be thirty-two before we can even think of having children."

"But Joe," Anna said, "you know it's everything I've

worked for." Like Joe, Anna left school at sixteen. Then she worked in boring office jobs for a few years. But she was really good with computers, and she'd worked hard to get a chance to go to university. She'd gone to classes and taken exams. Then at university, she did really well. "I can't believe you're saying this now," she added.

"I guess I thought, you know, that now you're leaving university . . ."

Anna didn't speak.

"It's not that I don't want you to do all this, Anna, you know that." Joe looked into her eyes. "I love you more than anything. Of course I want the best for you. It's just that I really want children, and I just think this is the best time. It's best to have kids before you're thirty."

They talked a little more, but couldn't agree. Finally, Joe said, "Well, I'm going to bed. Are you coming?"

"Not yet," Anna said. "I think I'll stay up and do some work."

Chapter 3

Eight days

"So how is the project going?" Professor Jensen asked. Anna was working on the project with Lisa and Ella. It was Wednesday afternoon, and the three of them were in the computer laboratory.

Ella was a very clever student, brilliant in fact. Her father, Leon Bridges, was quite a famous doctor. Ella had some interest in medicine, too, and could get information from her father. The goal of their project was to develop software to help doctors find a certain type of heart disease early. It was new and completely different from other software. The project was a secret, though, and only Professor Pam Jensen knew about it. Now she looked at the computer screens with interest.

"Mmm . . ." she said after a few minutes. "That looks very good. It looks like it could be ready by May 6."

"May 6?" Anna asked. "What's happening on May 6?"

The three of them looked at Professor Jensen.

"Well," she said, slowly, "I've been meaning to talk to you about this, but you remember that company I've been talking about, Synergy? I know Frank Hymes, the Head of Development there."

"Yes?"

"Well, they're interested, and they've agreed to listen to your presentation on May 6." Professor Jensen looked pleased with herself.

"Really?!"

"Yes, really," said Professor Jensen. "And if they like it, there's a chance they'll help the university to fund you to develop it for them."

"That's fantastic!" Lisa said.

"Incredible!" said Ella.

The three women jumped up and down with excitement.

"Now, wait a minute," the professor said, smiling. "I said *if*. They have to like it first."

"May 6?" Anna said. "But that's only . . ."

"Eight days." Professor Jensen finished Anna's sentence. Her pretty face was serious as she looked at the three of them. "So you've got a lot of work to do," she said.

◇◇◇

Twenty minutes after talking to Professor Jensen, Anna and Lisa were sitting at the Rainbow Cafe near the computer laboratory and having coffee.

"Wow!" Lisa said. "This is so exciting!"

"Yeah," said Anna. "Exciting." She sat with her face in her hands.

Lisa laughed. "You don't look very excited," she said. "What's the matter?" She looked into Anna's face. "Don't you think this will be great for us? We could have a contract to develop this software before we even finish university!"

"It's not that."

"Well, what is it?" asked Lisa.

"Oh, it's probably nothing . . ." Anna shook her head.

Rainbow Cafe

Lisa looked at her friend. "Nothing?" They both had a drink of their coffee.

"Well, it's Joe," Anna said finally. She sighed. She'd remembered yesterday's talk with her husband.

Lisa still didn't speak.

"It's just that he's decided that he wants children." Anna took a drink of coffee.

"I see. And you don't?" Lisa asked. "I thought you did." Lisa and Anna had first met two years ago, and they already knew a lot about each other.

"I do, I do . . ." Anna said. "Just not yet."

"You mean he wants them now?"

Anna told Lisa all about their visit to Chris and Lyn's, and about baby Billy. "I think Joe's been thinking about it for a long time," she said. "And I think he thought that when I left university . . . But now it seems I still may be busy for the next few years."

"It's probably just a feeling, you know, because of his brother's new baby," Lisa said. "It won't last."

"I'm not sure, Lisa," Anna said. "I think he just really wants to make a start before we get 'too old.'" She looked miserable.

"And you don't want to . . ."

"I want to do *this*, Lisa!" Anna said. "I think I'm good at it, and I want to really become successful at it. I mean, I spent years doing nothing really! I do want children, but they can wait!" Her voice was loud, and people started to look across at her from other tables.

"Children can wait," she said again, this time more softly.

Lisa touched Anna's hand gently. "Well, you're very good at it. Absolutely brilliant!"

Anna smiled. "And the thing is, Joe likes his job. It's a job, you know, but it's really not that important to him . . . he's more interested in having a family. And I'm more interested in my career—at least for now."

Lisa nodded. "You mean that he's more ready than you to have children now," she said.

"Yes," said Anna. "I think he is."

"So, what are you going to do?" asked Lisa.

Chapter 4

Talking

The next evening, about eight o'clock, Anna and Joe were both at home. Joe turned the sound down on the TV. "Did you think about what we talked about the other night?" he asked Anna.

"I'm sorry, Joe," Anna said, touching his head. "Let's talk about it later. I just have to work on this project. Professor Jensen wants us to give a presentation on it on May 6, and I haven't got everything I need yet!" She picked up her laptop and started off toward the little room she used as an office.

"But we need to talk, Anna," Joe said. "We have to see if we can find a way to do this. You can do that later, can't you?"

Anna sat down on the sofa, still holding her laptop. "OK, Joe," she said. "But I don't know what to say, really I don't."

"Well, listen," said Joe, gently. "I've thought about it a bit and I think I have a solution."

"Oh?"

"Well," said Joe, "I can try to move up at work, you know, try and get more money."

"Well, it's not a bad idea to do that anyway . . ."

"Then if you can take two or three years off now," Joe went on, "and have a baby, maybe two . . ."

"Two or three years!!"

"I know it seems like a long time, love," Joe said. "But think about it; you'll still be able to do your work after that."

"Joe!" Anna turned away. "I think you've gone mad or something. This project won't wait! I can't just leave this now. I may never get another opportunity to do what I really want to do, to have a career."

"But . . ."

She went on, "I've worked for years for this. I'm not going to stop now. I don't want to. Please don't ask me to." She looked at Joe like she didn't believe that he was saying all this.

"But, Anna," Joe said. "Be reasonable! We have to find a way to both get what we want."

"This is what we agreed, Joe," Anna said. "We talked about it a long time ago. What's changed?"

"*You've* changed," Joe said. "I thought you said when you left university, we could have kids. Instead, you're planning on working for years! I'm asking you for give-and-take."

"But this is 'I give and you take,' isn't it?" Anna laughed, but she was angry. "I have to give up my career for three years, more probably, and what do you give up?"

Joe jumped up. "I don't know how you can say that, Anna," he said. "I'm really trying to think this through."

Anna looked at him putting his hands through his curly brown hair. She suddenly became less angry. "I know, love," she said. "I know. It's just that it doesn't seem fair. Think about it from my point of view."

They were quiet for a few minutes, both of them thinking.

"Listen," said Anna. "This project I'm working on. Like I said, there's a very good chance we can sell the idea . . ."

"So?"

"So it will make us money," she said. "It means that later, when we have the children, we'll have enough."

"That may all take years, Anna," Joe said. "Anyway, I don't want money. I want a family. I want children."

"But this way we can have both!" Anna said. "Can't you see that?"

"Be reasonable, Anna!" Joe said.

"Reasonable?" Anna said, her voice louder. "I am being reasonable! We agreed to have children later, so that I could do this. Now you're the one who's saying 'let's change all that.' Who's the one who's being unreasonable?"

"I thought maybe when you left university, we could have kids," Joe said quietly. Then he said, "Can't we both be happy?"

Anna looked into Joe's lovely brown eyes. They looked so sad. "I don't know, love, I don't know," she said, shaking her head. "Now I really have to go and work on this project." She picked up her books and started walking toward her office.

"Well, at least think about it," said Joe as he watched her walk away.

Anna turned to look at him. "There's nothing to think about, Joe," she said. "Right now, I don't even know if I want children."

Anna closed the door of the office and took a deep

breath. She turned on her computer. She tried to work, but she couldn't. She found it hard to think about her project. She thought about Joe; she loved him so much.

But had things changed? Maybe they'd grown apart somehow. Was she so excited about her work at university that she didn't notice how he felt? Maybe she'd somehow missed the signs that he was unhappy.

She stared at her computer screen.

Chapter 5

Not a good day

Two days later, when Anna got back from the university, she saw that their car wasn't outside the house as usual. That was different, because Joe always drove to work, and he always got home first. She called "Hello, love!" as she walked through the door. But there was no reply. Funny, she thought. She walked into the living room, but Joe wasn't there. She found a note from him on the table.

Her heart jumped. She ran upstairs quickly, and into their bedroom. She looked in the wardrobe. A bag and some of his clothes were gone. She went in the bathroom. His toothbrush wasn't there either! Anna ran back into the bedroom, still holding the note. Joe! This was crazy! She couldn't believe that he'd left! What should she do? She ran downstairs and looked around the house and in the little garden. Was it some kind of joke? Then she realized it wasn't a joke at all. He really had gone! She went back to the bedroom, threw herself on the bed, and cried.

Sometime later, she heard a telephone ringing. She jumped up and ran to the phone. That was Joe, she was sure of it. He was calling to say he was OK!

"Hello, love," said the voice. It was Anna's mother. She called almost every day, just to say hello.

"Oh hi, Mom," Anna said. She felt disappointed that it wasn't Joe, but she tried to sound OK.

"What's wrong?" her mum asked. "You sound really upset."

Anna didn't feel like talking, but her mom's kind voice made her start crying again. She told her mom about Joe.

Irene Martin listened to her daughter, and then said, "I'm sorry, love. But if you ask me, it's just one of those things. It happens in marriage sometimes. He'll be back, you'll see. Joe loves you. Anyone can see that. And you love him!"

"I know, Mom," Anna said. "I do love him. Of course I do. But I don't know if it's enough. Honestly, I don't."

After talking to her mom, Anna really wanted to call Joe. But she stopped herself. She called Lisa instead, and told her about Joe and the note.

"I'm coming round," said Lisa.

"It's OK, Lisa," Anna said. "Really . . . I'll be alright."

"No problem," Lisa said. "I'll be there in twenty minutes."

When Lisa arrived, she hugged Anna. "Oh . . . I'm sorry, Anna," she said. She went into the kitchen and made some hot tea. Then the two of them sat talking in the living room.

"You know Joe, Lisa," Anna said. "Maybe he wants me to show him that I really love him or something. Do you think I should phone him? Ask him if we can talk?"

Lisa had met Joe a few times since Anna started at university. She'd been at their house for dinner a few times, and they'd all been to the pub together once or twice on a Friday evening. She liked him a lot. They got along really well. She thought for a minute.

"And if you talk . . . ?" she asked finally. "What are you going to say?"

"I'm not sure," Anna said.

"I think it's best to give him time," Lisa said. "While he's away from you, he'll realize even more how much he loves you."

"I don't know, Lisa," Anna said. "That's what my mom says, too, but maybe we've just grown apart. I mean I had no idea he felt so strongly about having children now! I guess I've been thinking so much about myself, about Cambridge, about this project, about everything."

"Don't blame yourself, Anna," Lisa said. "It's not you. These things happen. He's just realized that you're leaving university, but you'll still be busy. He'll come back, you'll see."

Anna looked at her friend. She wasn't so sure. "I don't know, Lisa. Really I don't."

Anna jumped up and walked across the room a few times. Then she turned to her friend. "Oh, what shall I do, Lisa?"

Lisa thought for a moment. Then she said, "Well, maybe what you need to do is to show him exactly how important your work is, and how good you are at it!"

"What do you mean?"

"Well, here's what you do . . ."

Chapter 6

The presentation

The next morning, Anna woke up early in the empty house and felt terrible. She got out of bed and went downstairs. She almost called Joe's cell phone, but she stopped herself. She put on the radio so that there was some noise in the house. Then she made herself some coffee and toast and got out of the house as quickly as she could.

During the day she really missed Joe, but she tried to concentrate on her work. The project presentation was in a few days, and Lisa and Ella needed her, she kept telling herself. She worked harder than ever, filling up the hours so that she didn't have to think about Joe. She'd known him since she was sixteen years old, and this was the longest time they'd ever been apart. When she got home, she expected to see him there. But he wasn't.

That evening, she called Chris and asked him to tell Joe about the presentation, as Lisa had suggested. It was a difficult conversation with Joe's brother. Chris was nice to her, but he really didn't know what to say.

"OK, Anna," he said. "I'll let him know."

She sat alone all evening, hoping that Joe would call back, but there was no word from him. She turned on the TV, but she couldn't concentrate. She tried to read, but she couldn't. She felt lost without Joe, and went to bed early. She missed talking to him, laughing with him. He was always so funny and just, well, he was Joe, and she loved him completely.

The days passed and the girls worked hard on getting everything ready. There was a lot to do; there was research to finish, programming to do, and the presentation to prepare.

The day before the presentation to Synergy came, Professor Jensen had suggested that the team, Anna, Lisa, and Ella, do a final practice of their presentation in front of her and some of the other computer science teachers.

The girls were nervous, but ready. They set up all their equipment, a computer and a screen, in the small room near the computer laboratory. Then Professor Jensen and the other five teachers came in and sat down. Anna wondered if Joe would come. Had Chris given him the message? Maybe he, Chris, had decided that it wasn't a good idea. Or maybe Joe had just decided not to come? Anna didn't know what to think.

"OK, girls. Carry on," said Professor Jensen.

The three of them stood on the stage, next to the projector, and looked at the group. "Good afternoon," said Ella. Ella and Lisa started with the basic idea of the project. It went well. Then, after about ten minutes, it was Anna's turn. She was the best presenter in the group, and her job was to talk about the details of the software they had started to develop, and how exactly it was going to help doctors find heart disease early.

Anna took a deep breath. She was nervous, but she started her presentation. Soon she was fine. She started to talk well, and went through her talk in a professional way. "And here," she said, pointing to one of the slides, "you can see how the software actually works."

Anna was calm on the outside, but inside she felt bad that Joe hadn't come.

Anna was about halfway through her talk when the door at the back of the room suddenly opened. Professor Jensen looked around, got up, and went toward the door to stop the person coming in. The presentation was secret, and other people couldn't enter the room.

As the door opened, Anna looked up and saw a head with brown curly hair look around the door. Then a tall, athletic figure walked in. It was Joe! Her heart jumped. "It's OK, Professor Jensen," she whispered. "It's my husband."

Professor Jensen let Joe into the room. He sat in the back row as Anna continued with her presentation. She tried to look only at the teachers, and not to look at Joe. She felt even more nervous now, but she knew her material well, and managed to get to the end.

". . . and that's why we think this software will be absolutely invaluable for the medical profession!" Anna finished.

The room went completely quiet. To Anna it seemed to last a long time, though it was only a few seconds. She looked at Lisa and Ella. Then she looked at the teachers nervously.

Suddenly, the teachers all stood up and clapped. "Thank you!" they said, one by one. They came up onto the stage to congratulate the girls.

"Wonderful!" one of them said.

"It was great! I think they'll love it," said another.

"Very exciting," said another. "Very, well . . . new!"

"Well done, all of you," said Professor Jensen. "That was excellent. I know tomorrow's going to be a great success."

Anna, Lisa, and Ella hugged each other, happy that everyone thought it was good.

One by one, the teachers started to leave. Anna looked up toward Joe. She felt her heart beating fast. He walked slowly down from the back row. Lisa and Ella started to leave the room as he came close to Anna.

"Hi," she said.

He smiled. "Hi."

"You got my message, then," she said.

Joe smiled. "Yes."

Anna and Joe walked outside into the little garden next to the building.

They didn't speak for a few moments. Both of them looked at the flowers.

"Lovely roses," said Joe.

Then Anna said, "I missed you."

"I missed you, too," said Joe.

It went quiet again.

Then Joe said, "Listen Anna. You're really good at this. I can see that. And I can really see how important this is to you, but I've got an idea . . ."

"Are you sure you want to talk about this again, Joe?" asked Anna. "We'll just argue about it. I don't want to fight anymore."

But Joe went on. "The thing is," he said, "I've had time to think about it. I can give up my job to look after the child . . . I really want to . . ."

Anna laughed. "Well, that's all very well," she said. "But what about actually having the child? It still means me taking time off to have the baby . . . at least three or four months. More, probably. How can I do that with all this going on?" She shook her head.

"Are you saying no?" asked Joe.

"I'm saying 'Think it through, Joe'," Anna said.

Joe took hold of Anna's hands and looked into her eyes. "Look, Anna," he said. "We have to find a way. While I've been away from you, I've realized one thing—you're the most important thing in the world to me. What's the most important thing in the world to you, is it me or your career? Because if doing things on a computer is more important to you than our relationship, then I don't think I can be with you anymore!"

Chapter 7

The choice

Anna stared at Joe, but she couldn't answer.

"I see," said Joe. He turned away from Anna and walked out of the garden. She watched him as he walked quickly down the street. She felt like she was frozen, and couldn't move. She wanted to call after him, but she didn't know what to say.

Anna stayed there for some time, just standing, alone. She looked at the place where Joe had been. She didn't realize the time, but she suddenly felt very cold. She went inside and got her coat, put it on, and started walking. She didn't think about where she was walking. She just knew that she didn't want to go home to that empty house; she just wanted to walk and think.

As she walked toward the city, Anna's thoughts went here, there, and everywhere. She thought about Joe and what he said about giving up his job. She thought about his question: what's the most important thing in the world to you? Oh, why did she have to choose? Couldn't she have both? It just wasn't fair. She thought about her presentation for Synergy tomorrow. Everyone thought it would be a great success. *Maybe Synergy will offer us money to develop this,* she thought. *And if they do, maybe . . .*

Could she find a way to keep Joe? Was there a way for both of them to be happy? A way to "give and take," as Joe said? She loved Joe with all her heart, but she knew that she was *meant* to work with computers. *Oh why is this happening to me now?* she asked herself. *Why now?*

She walked the streets of the city, not really noticing where she was. People were leaving work and going home, and the streets were busy with people rushing here and there. After about forty-five minutes of walking, Anna looked around and realized she wasn't far from Chris's house. She walked toward it, not really knowing what she would do when she got there. She just felt that something was pulling her there. She knew she had to go.

Anna went toward the house from the back. There was a wooden fence there, and she stood looking over the fence at the house in the pale afternoon light. In the garden, she could see figures, people. It was Joe, playing with Clara and Lizzie! The children were all over their uncle, pulling his hair, laughing and screaming. Anna could see that Joe was having a good time, too. She watched him for a few minutes. He looked happy with the kids, and she loved him so much. As she watched him, she realized something about Joe for the first time. She was meant to work with computers, and he was meant to be a father. He loved children, he was really good with them, and he wanted them more than anything. And because she loved him, she had to help him to do that. Somehow, she had to help him to be happy.

Suddenly, Joe looked up from the children and saw Anna. Anna smiled at him. He waved, quickly took the children inside, and ran over to her.

He opened the back door to let her in the garden. Then he held her tightly. He held her like he was frightened to let her go.

They didn't speak for a long time. They just stood there, holding each other.

Then he said, "Anna. My clever Anna."

"Joe."

"Yes?"

"I've been thinking about what you said," Anna said, "you know, about me taking a few months off to have a baby, then you stopping work."

"And?" Joe replied.

Anna kissed him and said, "I think we can give that a try."

Review: Chapters 1–4

A. Match the characters in the story to their descriptions. Use the names in the box.

Professor Jensen	Joe	Anna	Ella	Lisa	Chris	Clara

1. ____________ wants to start a family.
2. ____________ is the oldest student in her course.
3. ____________ is Joe's brother.
4. ____________ is Anna's niece.
5. ____________ is interested in medicine.
6. ____________ is working on a project with Anna and Ella.
7. ____________ is the only person who knows about the students' project.

B. Choose the best answer for each question.

1. Why do Anna and Joe go to Chris's house at the beginning of the story?

a. They visit them every week.

b. Chris and Lyn have a new baby.

c. Joe wants to talk to Chris.

d. They want to have dinner with them.

2. Why is Joe upset when Anna tells him about the project?

a. Because she is leaving the university.

b. Because he doesn't like the project.

c. Because Anna is going to work on the project after graduating.

d. Because he wants to do the project.

3. What is the project about?

a. Developing software to find heart disease early.

b. Developing medicine for heart disease.

c. Helping Ella's father.

d. Making secret software for the government.

4. What does Professor Jensen tell Anna, Lisa, and Ella?

a. The project isn't good enough.

b. They need to give their presentation on May 6.

c. They are going to get rich.

d. On May 6, her friend will come and help them.

C. Read each statement and circle whether it is true (T) or false (F).

1. Joe wants to have children while he and Anna are young. T / F

2. Anna met Joe when she was sixteen. T / F

3. Joe is now twenty-eight. T / F

4. Anna wants to have children later, when she's had a career. T / F

5. Lisa tells Anna to leave Joe. T / F

6. Joe thinks that Anna has changed. T / F

7. Anna doesn't love Joe any more. T / F

Review: Chapters 5–7

A. Complete each sentence using the correct word from the box.

children	garden	clap	cries	stage
presentation	calls	note	hugs	tightly

1. Anna reads the __________ that Joe leaves.
2. Anna lies on the bed and __________.
3. Anna's mom __________ her.
4. Lisa __________ Anna when she arrives at her house.
5. Anna asks Chris to tell Joe about her __________.
6. The three students stand on a __________ to give their presentation.
7. The teachers all __________ after the presentation.
8. Joe and Anna talk in the __________.
9. Anna watches Joe playing with Chris's __________.
10. Joe holds Anna __________ and they don't speak for a long time.

B. Choose the best answer for each question.

1. Where does Anna read the note?

a. in the kitchen

b. in the living room

c. in the bedroom

2. Why does Anna's mom call?

a. She calls almost every day.

b. She knows that Joe has gone.

c. She has a problem.

3. How does Anna feel being in her house alone?

a. OK b. happy c. terrible

4. How do Anna, Lisa, and Ella feel before the presentation?

a. confident b. nervous c. very happy

5. Who walks in in the middle of the presentation?

a. Joe b. Anna's mom c. Chris

6. What does Anna agree to do at the end of the story?

a. to leave Joe

b. to have children sooner

c. to spend more time with Chris's kids

C. Who said this? Choose the correct answer from the box.

Lisa	Anna	Joe	Anna's mom

1. "It happens in marriage sometimes." __________

2. "Well, here's what you do . . ." __________

3. "You're the most important thing in the world to me." __________

4. "I think we can give that a try." __________

D. What do you think will happen after the end of the story? Choose from the options below or add your own ideas.

1. Anna will start on the project, leave for a few months to have a baby, then go back to the project. Joe will then leave his job and look after the baby.

2. Anna will start on the project, leave for a few months to have a baby, then go back to the project. Anna's mom will then look after the baby.

3. Anna will leave the project and have children. In a few years, she will try to find a job in computer science.

4. Anna will leave the project, have children, and never work again. Joe will keep his job.

5. Your own ideas: ____

____

Answer Key

Chapters 1–4

A:

1. Joe; **2.** Anna; **3.** Chris; **4.** Clara; **5.** Ella; **6.** Lisa; **7.** Professor Jensen

B:

1. b; **2.** c; **3.** a; **4.** b

C:

1. T; **2.** T; **3.** F; **4.** T; **5.** F; **6.** T; **7.** F

Chapters 5–7

A:

1. note; **2.** cries; **3.** calls; **4.** hugs; **5.** presentation; **6.** stage; **7.** clap; **8.** garden; **9.** children; **10.** tightly

B:

1. b; **2.** a; **3.** c; **4.** b; **5.** a; **6.** b

C:

1. Anna's mom; **2.** Lisa; **3.** Joe; **4.** Anna

D:

Answers will vary.

Background Reading:

Spotlight on . . . Childcare across cultures

Different cultures often have different ways of raising children, and caring for them when they are young.

In some Asian countries, for example, it is quite common for the extended family to be involved in the child's care. So grandparents, aunts, and uncles often play a big role. It is also more common to have "live-in help"—a nanny or domestic helper who looks after the baby or young child.

In western societies, having "live-in help" is less common. When both mother and father go out to work, the young child may be sent to a special daycare nursery. Some countries, such as Sweden, have generous childcare facilities. Most public nurseries are open from 6 a.m. until 6 p.m., and some even provide overnight and weekend services.

Having a baby often means a change in lifestyle for both women and men in all cultures. They have some choices to make, especially if both of them work. Do they stop work to look after the baby full-time? Do they leave the baby with a relative? Do they hire a nanny or babysitter? Is there a good nursery where they can send the baby? Suddenly, life becomes a little different!

Think About It

1. Is it usual in your country for both parents to work?
2. Is it common in your country for grandparents and other relatives to look after the baby or small child?

Glossary

adult	(*n.*)	a person who is fully grown
career	(*n.*)	an occupation or profession
concentrate	(*v.*)	to think carefully
contract	(*n.*)	a written agreement
develop	(*v.*)	to help something grow
fence	(*n.*)	a barrier enclosing a field or garden
graduate	(*v.*)	to leave school with a degree or diploma
heart disease	(*n.*)	a problem with the heart that affects its normal functioning
kid/kids	(*n.*)	children (slang)
laptop	(*n.*)	a portable computer
presentation	(*n.*)	a verbal report
project	(*n.*)	a long-term assignment
reasonable	(*adj.*)	sensible and moderate; not extreme (opposite: *unreasonable*)